CONSERVATORY CANADA™

New Millennium Voice Series

GRADE THREE

Editorial Committee
D.F. Cook
Elizabeth Parsons
Anita Ruthig

With thanks to Lisa Martin, Jennifer Floris, and Debra Wanless for their assistance.

Official Examination Repertoire List Pieces and Studies of Conservatory Canada - Grade 3

*Publication of the New Millennium Voice Series is made possible
by a generous grant from Dr. Don Wright.*

© 1999 Conservatory Canada
Published and Distributed by Novus Via Music Group Inc.
All Rights Reserved.

ISBN 978-0-88909-191-7

Novus Via Music Group Inc.
189 Douglas Street, Stratford, Ontario, Canada N5A 5P8
(519) 273-7520 www.NVmusicgroup.com

cover design:
Robin E. Cook, AOCA

About the Series

The *New Millennium Voice Series* is the official repertoire for Conservatory Canada examinations. This graded series, in eight volumes (Grade 1 to Grade 8), is designed not only to serve the needs of teachers and students for examinations, but it is also a valuable teaching resource and comprehensive anthology for any singer. The List Pieces have been carefully selected and edited, and represent repertoire from the Baroque, Classical, Romantic/Impressionist, and 20th-century periods. In addition, each volume includes the syllabus requirements for the grade, a graded arrangement of *O Canada* (with words in English and French), and a Glossary containing a short biography of each composer. Conservatory Canada requires that at least one Canadian composition be performed in every examination. Composers working in Canada are well represented in the series. A small asterisk next to their name identifies them. Photographs of some Canadian composers are included with the biography.

Notes on Editing

Most composers in the Baroque and Classical periods included only sparse dynamic, articulation, tempo and other performance indications in their scores. Where we felt it necessary, we have added suggested markings. The *New Millennium Series* is not an Urtext edition. All editorial markings are intended to be helpful suggestions rather than a final authority. The choice of tempo is a matter of personal taste, technical ability, and appropriateness of style. Most of our suggested metronome markings are expressed within a range of tempi. In the 19th and 20th centuries, composers included more performance indications in their scores, and as a consequence, fewer editorial markings have been required.

No markings have been used to suggest phrasing and breathing. In accordance with Conservatory Canada's policy regarding redundant accidentals, we have followed the practice that a barline cancels accidentals. Unnecessary accidentals following the barline have been used only in exceptional circumstances.

Bearing in mind acceptable performance practices, you are free to use your own judgement, musicianship and imagination in changing any editorial marking, especially in the areas of dynamics, articulation, and phrasing.

Every effort has been made to identify the authorship of texts and translations. Where we have not been able to confirm that the authorship is generally accepted as being anonymous, we have used the term "unknown".

The pieces in the *New Millennium Series* have been chosen as an introduction to enjoyable repertoire that is fun to sing while, at the same time, helps to develop your technique and musicianship. We hope you will explore the broad variety of styles and periods represented in this book. It is important that you learn as many pieces as possible before deciding which ones you will sing in the examination.

London, Ontario
September 1999

The Conservatory Canada Voice Syllabus gives full details regarding examinations. Teachers, students, and parents are advised to consult the most recent Syllabus for current requirements, regulations, procedures and deadline for application.

GRADE 3 - Table of Contents

Indicates Canadian Composer

A BREEZE COMES DANCING

Irene Gass

Arthur Baynon
(20th Century)

A breeze comes dan-cing o'er the hills, A ze-phyr light and gay;_____ She stirs the dream-ing buds and leaves, And calls them out to play;_____ "Wake up! Wake up! come, sleep no more, For

spring now knocks on win – ter's door." Sweet spring is at hand._____ Sweet

spring_____ is at hand._____ Up

colla voce . . . . *mf* *rit.* *mp*

a tempo

– on my wings she'll proud – ly ride, A – cross the wa – king world,_____ 'Mid

a tempo

3

op' - ning flow'rs and birds on wing, 'Neath beau - ty's flag_ un furled;_____ And

fox - glove bells, with gold - en tongue, Shall ring a peal, while all things young sing

greet - ing to spring_____ sing greet - ing to Spring._____

colla voce

calando

THE SANDMAN
Sandmännchen

Anonymous
English version by J. Michael Diack

Johannes Brahms
(1833-1897)

Andante ♩ = 50-60

Be - neath the sil - v'ry moon - light, Like
birds you heard this morn - ing Have
comes the lit - tle sand - man, In

ti - ny spark - ling gems, The flow - 'rets all are
long___ since gone___ to rest, And now are close to -
ev - 'ry house___ he'll peep, To find the lit - tle

5

slum - ber,__ my__ dar - ling__ ba - by dear!

dear!

2. The
3. Now

SING LULLABY

Anonymous

Attributed to William Byrd
(c1542-1623)
arr. D.F. Cook

My sweet lit – tle dar – ling, my com – fort and joy, Sing lul – la – by lul – la, In beau – ty sur – pass – ing the

8

prin - ces of Troy, Sing lul - la - by lul - la;

cresc.

Now hush, child, now sleep, child, thy mo - ther's sweet

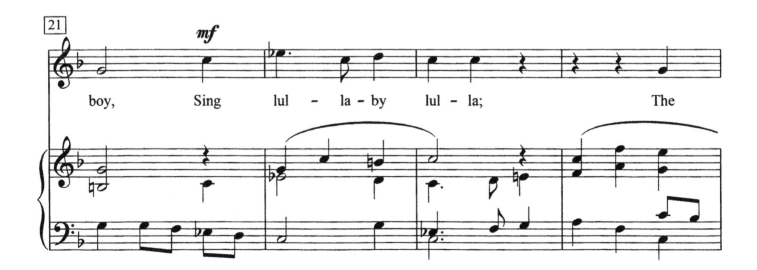

mf

boy, Sing lul - la - by lul - la; The

Gods bless and keep thee from cru – el an – noy, Sing

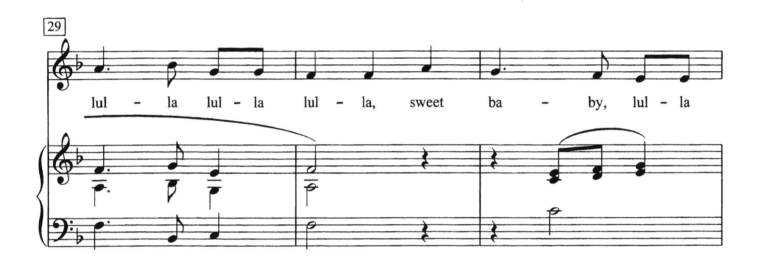

lul – la lul – la lul – la, sweet ba – by, lul – la

lul – la, sweet ba – by, lul – la – by lul – la.

THE MOCKING BIRD

Traditional (Appalacian)

American Folksong
arr. R. Fleming

Freely, with expression ♩ = 56-63

Hush lit – tle ba – by don't say a word; Pop – pa's gon – na buy you a mock – ing bird.

If that mock – ing bird can't sing, Pop – pa's gon – na buy you a

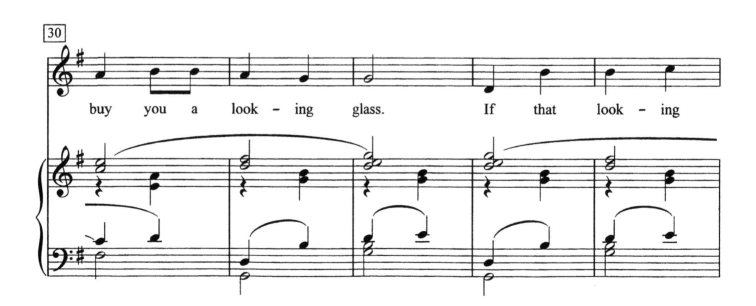

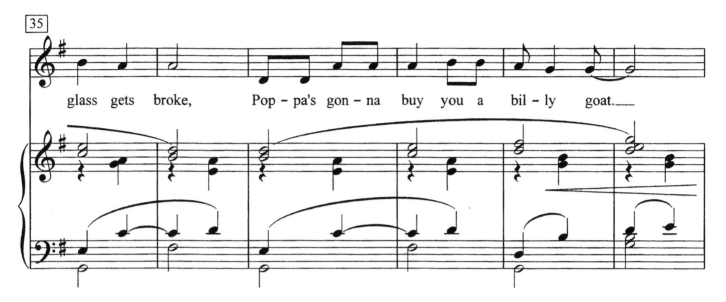

glass gets broke, Pop – pa's gon – na buy you a bil – ly goat.___

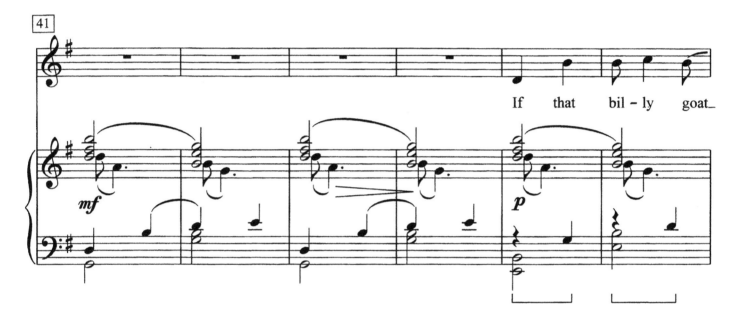

If that bil – ly goat___

— don't pull, Pop – pa's gon – na buy you a cart and bull.

cresc. *f*

If that cart and bull turn o - ver, Pop - pa's gon - na

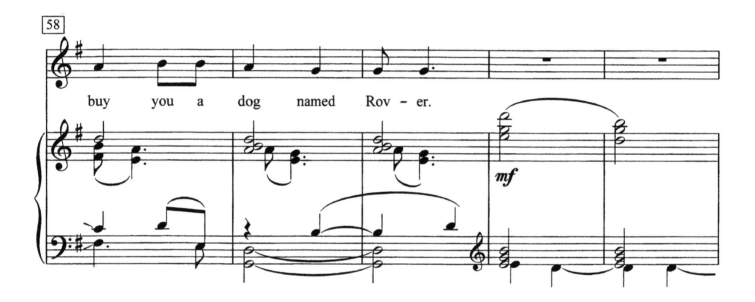

buy you a dog named Rov - er.

mf

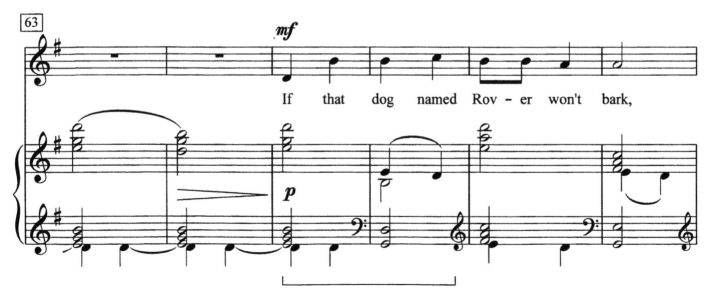

mf

If that dog named Rov - er won't bark,

p

Pop – pa's gon – na buy you a horse and cart. If that horse and

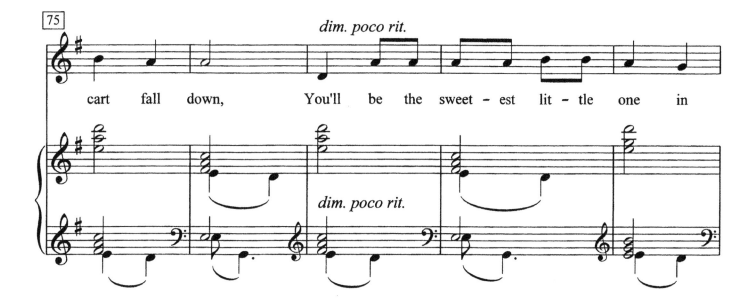

cart fall down, You'll be the sweet – est lit – tle one in

town._____

GREEN NOW THE MOUNTAIN-SIDE

Traditional (Tyrolese)
English version by H. Perrin

Austrian Folksong
arr. D. F. Cook

© 1999 D.F. Cook

A LA CLAIRE FONTAINE

Traditional (Québec)
English version by R. Keith Hicks

*Canadian Folksong
arr. G. Coutts

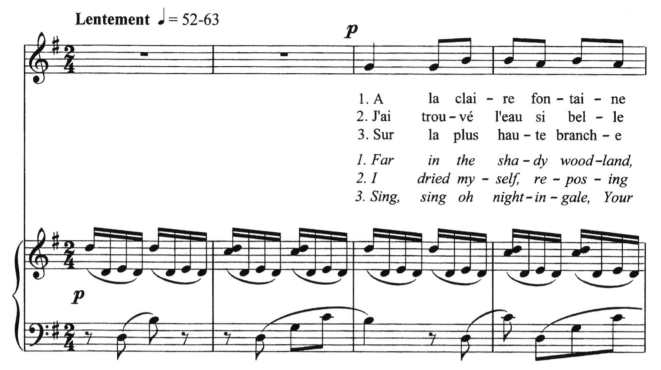

18

Que je m'y suis bai – gné.
Je me suis fait sé – cher. Lui y'a long – temps que je t'ai – me
Toi qui as le coeur gai.

That *I plunged* *in* *to swim.*
Sang *night – in – gale* *to* *me.* *Since* *dawn of* *day* *I've__* *wait – ed*
Mine *can* *but* *pine* *a – way.*

Ja – mais je ne t'ou – blie – rai.

for *her* *my__* *heart's own* *love.*

THE LARK IN THE MORN

Traditional (England)

British Folksong
arr. Cecil J. Sharp

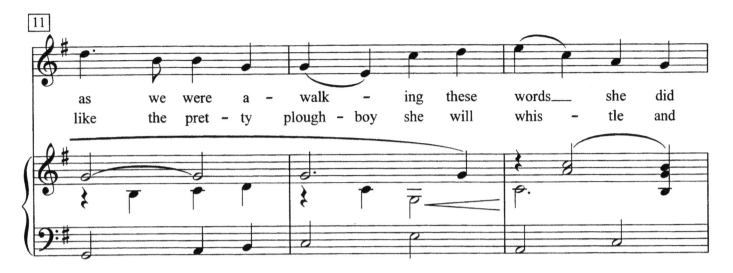

11

as   we   were   a —   walk —   ing   these   words___   she   did
like   the   pret —   ty   plough – boy   she   will   whis —   tle   and

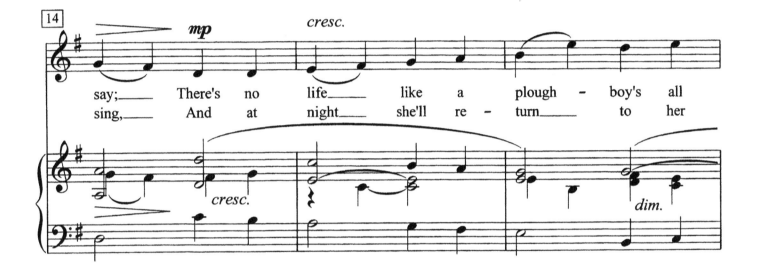

14   *mp*   *cresc.*

say;___   There's   no   life___   like   a   plough —   boy's   all
sing,___   And   at   night___   she'll   re —   turn___   to   her

cresc.   *dim.*

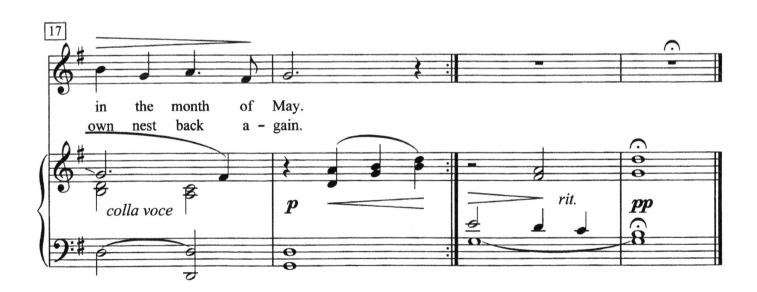

17

in   the   month   of   May.
own   nest   back   a – gain.

colla voce   *p*   *rit.*   *pp*

21

LITTLE RED BIRD

Traditional (Isle of Man)

British Folksong
arr. Mitchell & Biss

Lit - tle red bird of the lone - ly moor,

Lone - ly moor, lone - ly moor, Lit - tle red bird of the

lone - ly moor, O where did you sleep_ last night?_____

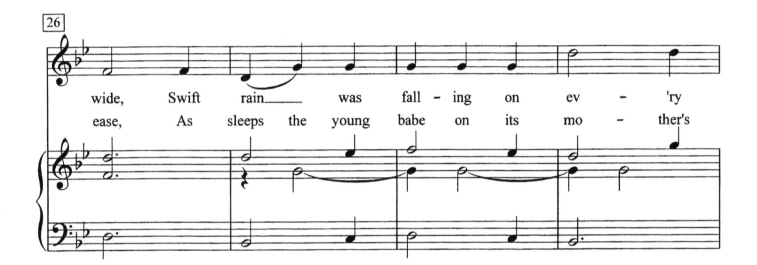

CRADLE SONG

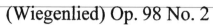
(Wiegenlied) Op. 98 No. 2

English version by J. Michael Diack

Franz Schubert
(1797-1828)

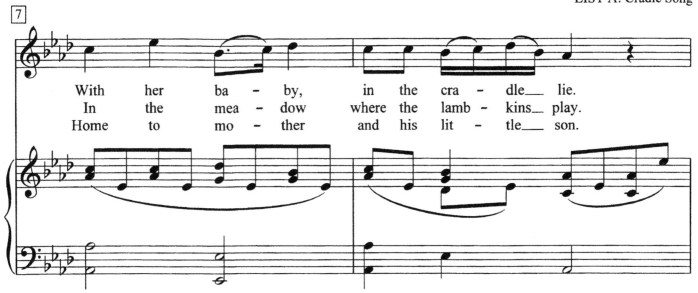

With her ba – by, in the cra – dle__ lie.
In the mea – dow where the lamb – kins__ play.
Home to mo – ther and his lit – tle__ son.

AUPRÈS DE MA BLONDE

Traditional (Québec)
English translation by Harold Heiberg

*Canadian Folksong
arr. P. Creston

CHILD OF THE UNIVERSE

Craig Cassils

*Craig Cassils
(1950-   )

1. The sun is on-ly a star,___

- dren now.___ That's where I fit in.___

rit.

LULLABY

Christina Rossetti

*Keith Bissell
(1912-1992)

SNOW FLAKES

Mary Mapes Dodge

Frederick H. Cowen
(1852-1935)

When - e'er a snow - flake leaves the sky, It turns and

turns, to say "good – bye! Good – bye dear cloud, so cool and

gray, Good – bye dear cloud, so cool and gray" Then

light - ly trav - els on its way   And when a

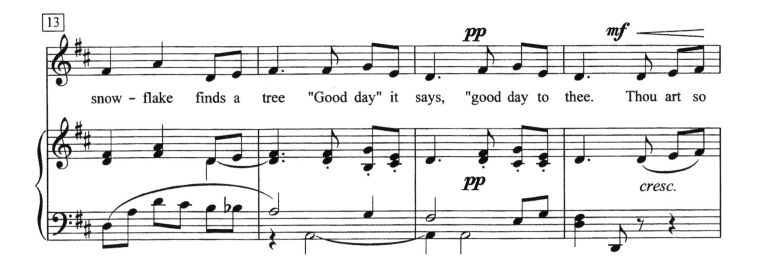

snow - flake finds a tree "Good day" it says, "good day to thee. Thou art so

bare and lone - ly, dear, Thou art so bare and lone - ly

20 slower

dear. I'll rest, and call my com - rades here."

23 a tempo *mf*

But when a snow - flake, brave and meek, Lights on a

26 *cresc.*   *p*

lit - tle maid - en's cheek. It starts "how

warm and soft the day, how warm and soft the day, 'Tis

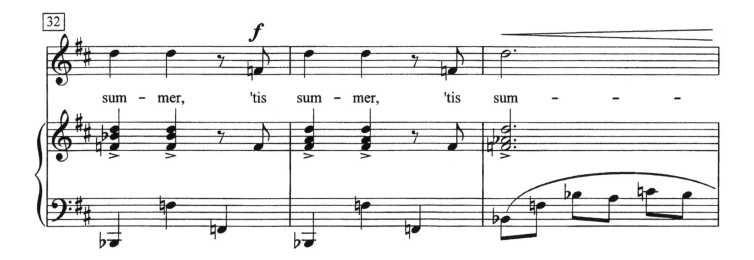

sum - mer, 'tis sum - mer, 'tis sum - - - -

mer." And it melts a - way.

WISHES

Clifford Crawley

*Clifford Crawley
(1929-   )

some of them just re- main wish- es,_____ And may - be it's

bet – ter they do_____ For wish – es are great fun to

poco allargando

wish,_____ But wish – es that I wish to - day

poco allargando

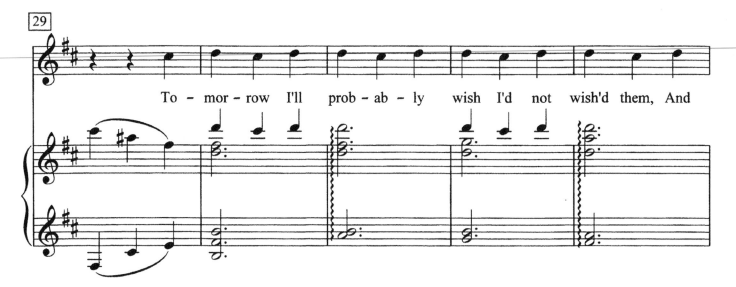

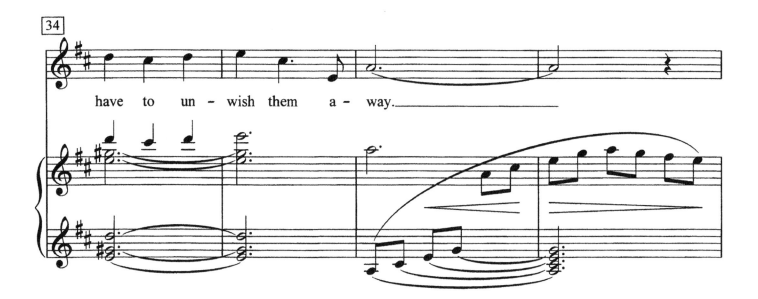

of – ten wish wish – es, I of – ten wish wish – es, I'm sure that you

wish wish – es too;_____ So I wish that some of the

best of those wish – es That you wish'd, will come true for you.

rit.

THE FATE OF GILBERT GIM

Mary Lynn Williamson

*Margaret Drynan
(1915-1999)

With drama and rubato ♩ = 72-80

mf

When Gil – bert Ga – ry Gro – ver Gim was

search – ing for his dog, He found his feet were lead – ing him to-

wards the goo – ky bog. When land had end – ed he did leap from

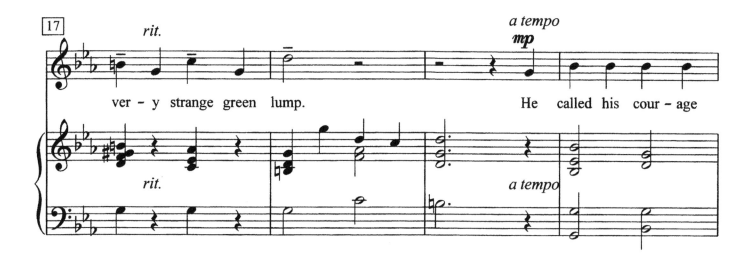

Gro - ver Gim jumped on the lump's green back. Then

accel. e cresc.

life sprang to its mot - tled hide and part of it did

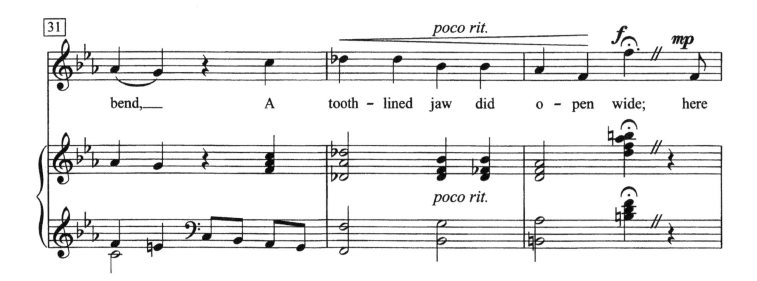

poco rit.

bend,___ A tooth - lined jaw did o - pen wide; here

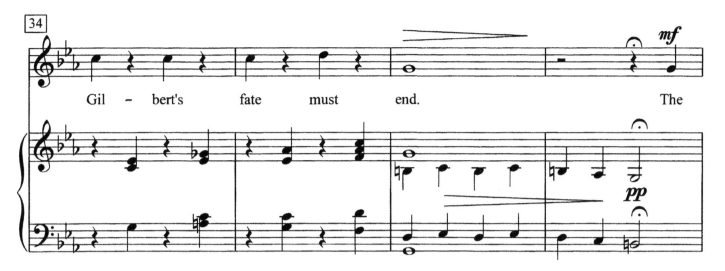

Gil – bert's fate must end. The

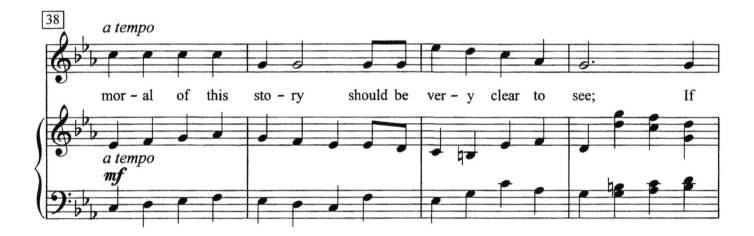

mor – al of this sto – ry should be ver – y clear to see; If

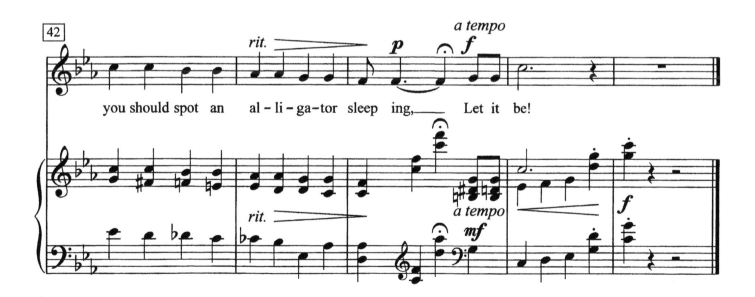

you should spot an al – li – ga – tor sleep ing,___ Let it be!

THE CROOKED MAN

Traditional

*Cyril Hampshire
(1900-1963)

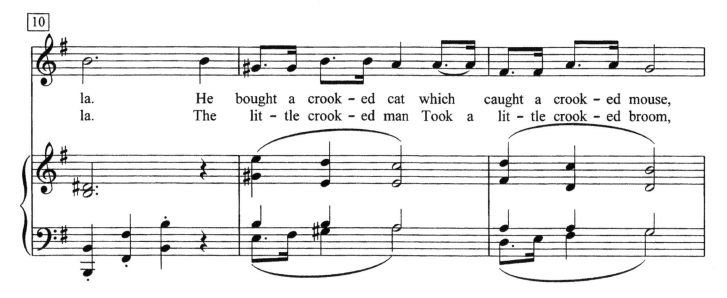

la. He bought a crook – ed cat which caught a crook – ed mouse,
la. The lit – tle crook – ed man Took a lit – tle crook – ed broom,

Fa la, la, la, la, la And they all lived to – geth – er in a
Fa la, la, la, la, la And he swept them both a – way to an

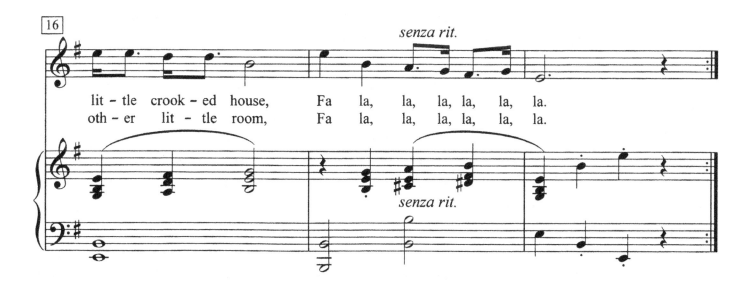

senza rit.

lit – tle crook – ed house, Fa la, la, la, la, la, la.
oth – er lit – tle room, Fa la, la, la, la, la, la.

senza rit.

49

TWO KITES AND A RAIN CLOUD

Helen Isobel Bond

*Burton Kurth
(1890-1977)

Andante ♩ = 84-96

Two lit – tle Kites one win – dy day sail'd__ up in – to the sky; when they look'd down I heard them say: "How could we fly, oh! fly so

high?" So they in won - der, won - der cry. A pass - ing

cloud call'd out to them; "Hold on to me, hold on, my dears! I'll bring you

down, down, down to earth up - on my heav'n - ly tears."

SUN TWINKLES

from *Songs That Touch The Heart*

R. Barry Gosse

R. Barry Gosse
(1936-1988)
arr. A.D. Wood

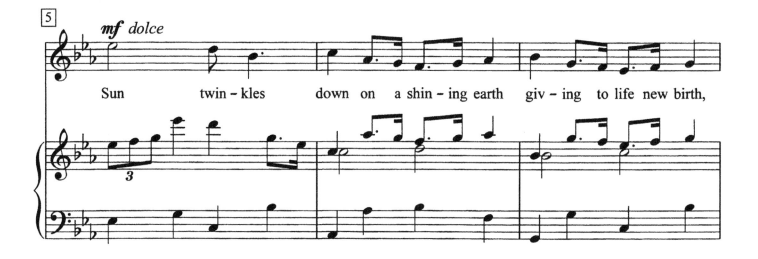

Sun twin-kles down on a shin-ing earth giv-ing to life new birth,

Wel - come Spring. High in the leaf - y trees, rob - ins sing.

Love danc – es down to touch ev – ry – thing. Wav – ing, sway – ing,

breez – es sigh My heart leaps up to meet the sky.

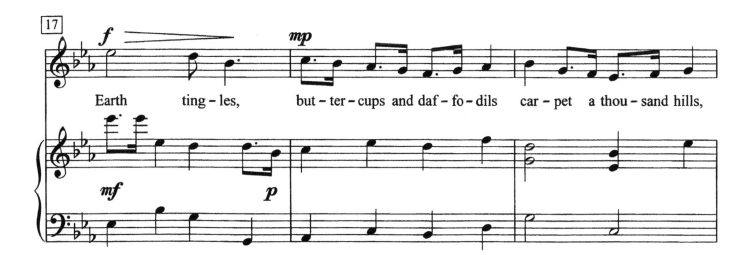

Earth ting – les, but – ter – cups and daf – fo – dils car – pet a thou – sand hills,

Sun – sets gleam, Soft fur – ry crea – tures curl up to sleep.

God's lit – tle child – ren have dreams to keep, Spring_ has come_ to ev' – ry part.

There's mus – ic sing-ing round my heart, There's sun – shine twink – ling in my heart.

GLORIA DEO
from *Carol Cantata*

Anonymous

*David Ouchterlony
(1914-1987)

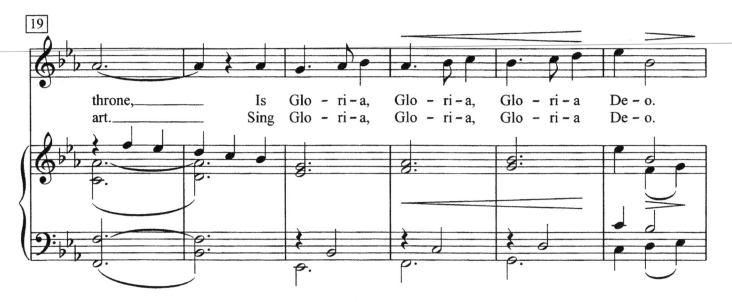

throne,_____ Is Glo - ri - a, Glo - ri - a, Glo - ri - a De - o.
art._____ Sing Glo - ri - a, Glo - ri - a, Glo - ri - a De - o.

King of the whole earth, King of my own!
King of the whole earth, King of my heart!

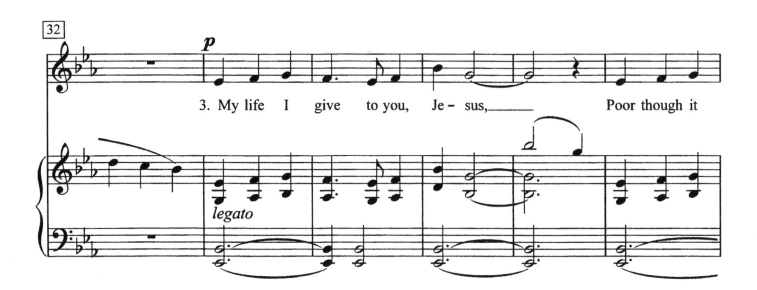

3. My life I give to you, Je - sus,_____ Poor though it

legato

is, no long-er mine._____ What I can do, my Lord Je-sus, I

prom-ise, my life will be guid-ed by Thine._____ Sing Glo-ri-a,

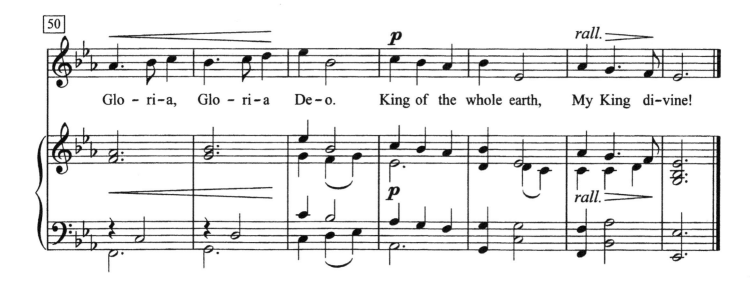

Glo-ri-a, Glo-ri-a De-o. King of the whole earth, My King di-vine!

THE SCARECROW

Warren Smith

Warren Smith
(1885-1971)

Oh, he looks for - lorn,_____ for -
For he stands on guard,_____ on

lorn,_____
guard._____

And he nev - er says a word.
And he nev - er says a

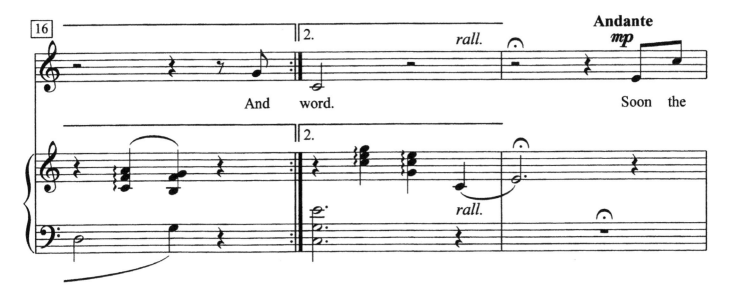

And word.

Soon the

61

19 birds come down just to steal the seed.___ Black ones, brown ones,

Tempo primo

22 what a jol – ly feed! But they soon take fright, as in – deed they might,

25 Though he nev – er speaks a word.___ All a – long his arms are

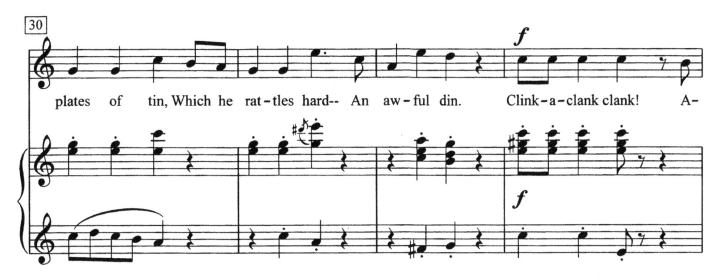

plates of tin, Which he rat-tles hard-- An aw-ful din. Clink-a-clank clank! A-

way they fly, Clink-a-clank clank, And he grins Good-bye!

For he's a Scare-crow!

LOVE DIVINE, ALL LOVES EXCELLING

Charles Wesley

*Bert Vander Hoek
(1936-   )

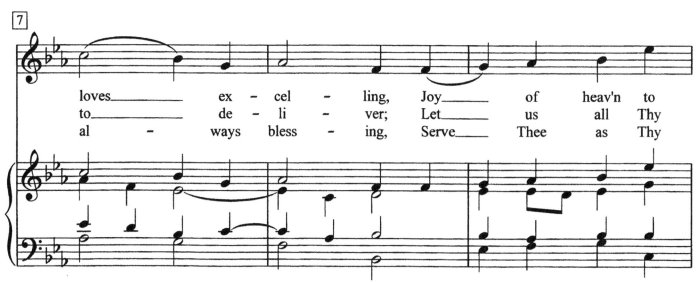

64

Lyrics:
Love Divine, all loves excelling, Joy of heav'n to
Come Almighty to deliver; Let us all Thy
Thee we would be always blessing, Serve Thee as Thy

10

earth   come   down,   Fix_____ in us_____
grace   re –   ceive;   Sud – den – ly_____
hosts   a –   bove,   Pray,_____ and   praise_____

13

_____ Thy   hum – ble   dwel –   ing,_____ All_____ Thy
_____ re – turn   and   ne –   ver,_____ Ne – ver
_____ Thee,   with – out   cea –   sing,_____ Glo – ry

16

faith –   –   –   ful   mer – cies   crown.
more_____ Thy   tem – ples   leave.
in_____ Thy   per – fect   love.

THE DAY BEFORE CHRISTMAS

Nancy Telfer

*Nancy Telfer
(1950-)

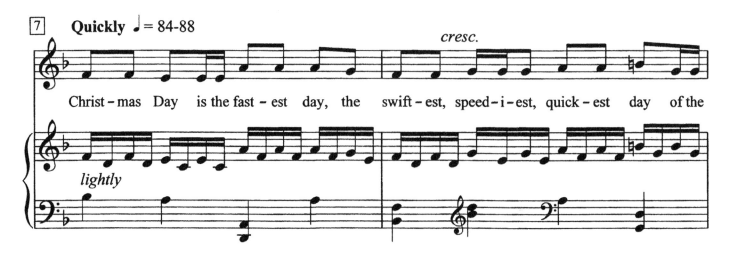

year. On Christ-mas Day, the time sweeps by... It

flies through the air: it climbs to the sky... It

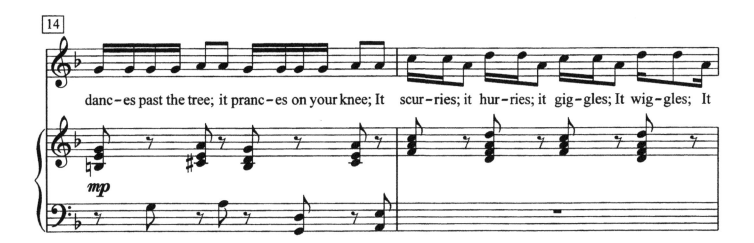

danc-es past the tree; it pranc-es on your knee; It scur-ries; it hur-ries; it gig-gles; It wig-gles; It

gig – gles, wig – gles. For Christ – mas Day is the fast – est day, the

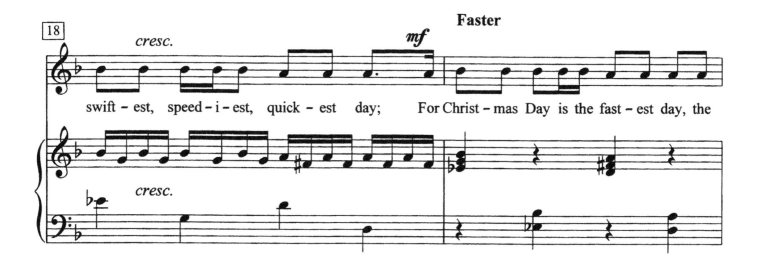

swift – est, speed – i – est, quick – est day; For Christ – mas Day is the fast – est day, the

swift-est, the speed-i-est, the quick-est day____ of the year.

GLOSSARY
Compiled by Debra Wanless

About the Composers in Grade Three

BAYNON, Arthur. A British composer of whom little is known.

*BISSELL, Keith (1912-1992). Canada. Keith

Bissell was born in Meaford, Ontario and became a composer, educator, conductor and lecturer. He studied composition at the University of Toronto and was supervisor of school music in Edmonton (1949-55), where he also was an organist and choirmaster. In 1955, he moved to Scarborough (near Toronto), Ontario to become supervisor of school music there. He was a tireless supporter of Canadian composers and worked hard to promote their music. He arranged Canadian folk songs for voice, choir and piano and also wrote orchestral, chamber, choral and vocal music and works for the stage.

BLISS, Arthur (1891-1975). Britain. Bliss was born in London and studied at Cambridge University and at the Royal College of Music with Charles Stanford and Vaughan Williams. He lived for a short time in California and wrote symphonies, ballets, film music and piano works. Bliss eventually returned to England and became music director for the BBC. The King bestowed a knighthood upon him in 1950, and three years later, Sir Arthur Bliss was appointed by the new Queen Elizabeth II to the distinguished position of Master of the Queen's Musick.

BRAHMS, Johannes (1833-1897). Germany. Brahms was the son of a double-bass player who was also his first teacher. Although his parents originally hoped that Brahms would become an orchestral player, they soon realized that he was a very gifted pianist. His early performing experiences were limited to playing in taverns and saloons, but a concert tour with the great Hungarian violinist Joachim greatly advanced his career. A friend of Schumann and Liszt, Brahms also established himself as a skilled composer. He wrote many songs (called *Lieder* in German) using words by the great German poets, and arranged many German folk songs and composed symphonies and choral works.

BYRD, William (1543-1623). Britain. William Byrd is perhaps the most important English composer who lived and worked in the reign of Queen Elizabeth I. Very little is known of his early years, but we do know that at the age of 20 he was appointed organist of Lincoln Cathedral and that by then he had composed some choral music. In 1570, he accepted a position with the Chapel Royal and moved to London. Though he composed music for instrumental ensembles and for keyboard, he is best remembered for his sensitive settings of the English language in his many choral pieces and solo songs.

*CASSILS, Craig (born 1950). Canada. Craig

Cassils was born in Deloraine, Manitoba, graduated from Brandon University and now teaches music at Elmdale School in Steinbach. In the school and in the community, he works with children's choirs, church choirs, and musical theatre. Cassils has composed a great deal of vocal music for young people. Most exciting is the new musical for young voices, "2000 Together," a collaboration with Robin Richardson. Craig is probably best known for his popular *Child of the Universe* and *Clowns*.

*COOK, Donald F. (born 1937). Canada. Donald

Cook grew up and received his early musical training in St. John's, Newfoundland. After further studies in New York City and London, England, Dr. Cook returned to Newfoundland to become the founding director of the School of Music at Memorial University. Since 1992, he has served as Principal of Western Ontario Conservatory (now Conservatory Canada). Most of Dr. Cook's compositions are for solo voice or choir, and many are based on Canadian folk songs.

*COUTTS, George James (1888-1962). Canada. Coutts was born in Aberdeen, Scotland and held a post as an organist by the age of 14. He moved to Canada in 1911, first settling in Toronto where he worked as an organist, pianist, conductor, composer, teacher and adjudicator. In 1921 he moved to Regina, Saskatchewan to become head of piano at the Regina Conservatory. From 1931 to 1940 Coutts lived in Vancouver, British Columbia, after which time he returned to Toronto to teach at the Royal Conservatory of Music and the University of Toronto. His works include music for piano, organ, violin, choir and solo voice. He arranged the folk song collection, *Douze Chansons Canadiennes*, published in 1958.

COWEN, Frederick Hymen (1852-1935). Britain. Although Cowen was born in Jamaica, his family moved to England when he was an infant. He showed an early interest in composition; he had a waltz published by the age of 6, and completed his first operetta when he was 8. A gifted pianist and conductor, Cowen studied in Leipzig and Berlin. His works are of variable quality and include ballads, sacred songs, orchestral works, operas, oratorios and cantatas. He received a knighthood for his work in music.

*CRAWLEY, Clifford (born 1929). Canada. Born  and educated in England, where he studied with composers Lennox Berkeley and Humphrey Searle. Crawley taught music in elementary and secondary schools before moving to Canada in 1973. He is a Professor Emeritus of Queen's University in Kingston, Ontario, where he taught from 1973 to 1993. He now resides in Toronto where he continues to compose and work as a music consultant, choir director, adjudicator, examiner and composer. Crawley has written more than 80 compositions, at times using the pen name Clifford Curwin. His works, many of which are intended for young players, include piano duets, operas, chamber works, and many pieces for band, orchestra and choir. Crawley is an active participant in the "Creating Music in the Classroom" and "Artists in the Schools" programs in Ontario.

CRESTON, Paul (1906-1985). U.S.A. Paul Creston was born in New York City as Joseph Guttoveggio. His parents were Italian immigrants who could not afford his education beyond elementary school. Although he had some organ and piano lessons, he was largely a self-taught composer. In 1934 he took an organist post and in 1938 won the Guggenheim Fellowship. In his compositions, Creston sometimes borrows elements of the Impressionist composers and often uses modal harmonies. His compositions include piano works, 5 symphonies, 12 concertos and choral works.

*DRYNAN, Margaret (1915-1999). Canada. Margaret Drynan was born and educated in Toronto, Ontario. Her teachers included Michael Head and Healey Willan and she sang for many years in Willan's church choir. Much of her career was spent in Oshawa, Ontario where she was a music consultant for the Durham Region Board of Education. She still found time to compose music and to play an active role in the Royal Canadian College of Organists. Her pieces include a Missa Brevis, four operettas, and over 40 songs and folksong arrangements.

*FLEMING, Robert (1921-1976). Canada. Fleming  was a composer, pianist, organist, choirmaster and teacher who was born in Prince Albert, Saskatchewan, but moved with his family to Saskatoon when he was 8. His first music lessons were with his mother but he later studied in England with Arthur Benjamin and Herbert Howells and in Toronto with Healey Willan. For much of his professional life Fleming was the music director for the National Film Board. He wrote ballets, 250 film scores, orchestral and band works, 25 chamber works, piano and organ pieces, choral music, hymns, carols and songs. He moved to Ottawa in 1970 where he worked as a teacher and church musician until his death.

*GOSSE, R. Barry (1936-1988). Canada. Gosse  was a piano virtuoso at the age of eleven. Following graduation from the University of Toronto, he attended the Eastman School of Music in Rochester, N.Y. Gosse spent most of his career as a school music teacher and music consultant in Toronto. He also served as conductor of both the Etokicoke Centennial Choir and the Etobicoke Youth Orchestra.

*HAMPSHIRE, Cyril (1900-1963). Canada. Hampshire was a pianist, choir conductor, adjudicator and composer born in Wakefield, England. He was an assistant organist at the age of 14 and studied at Leeds College. Hampshire came to Canada in 1921 and lived for a time in Moose Jaw, Saskatchewan. In 1939 he became Principal of the Hamilton Conservatory of Music in Hamilton,

Ontario. Six years later he accepted an appointment as director of music for the Hamilton public schools. It is therefore not surprising that he composed or arranged songs for school children, and also compiled the useful book *An Introduction to Practical Sight Singing* (1951).

*KURTH, Burton (1890-1977). Canada. Kurth  was a singer, educator, composer and organist who was born in Buffalo, New York. He studied in New York, Winnipeg and Chicago, settling in Winnipeg in 1909 to teach singing. He moved to Vancouver in 1927 where he had a long career as church organist and supervisor of music for Vancouver schools. Kurth composed many songs for use in schools and also compiled several collections including *Little Songs for Little People*, *Music Makers*, and *Sing Me a Song*. His book *Sensitive Singing* offers advice to young singers.

MITCHELL, Donald (born 1925). Britain. Donald Mitchell is a music critic and musicologist, specializing in modern music. He has edited biographies on W.A Mozart and Benjamin Britten and has written a three-volume series on the music of Gustav Mahler. Mitchell is the founder and editor of the music periodical *Music Survey* is also the director of the Faber Music Company.

*OUCHTERLONY, David (1914-1987). Canada.  Dr. Ouchterlony was born in Guelph, Ontario and was an organist, choirmaster, teacher, administrator and adjudicator. A pupil of Healey Willan, Dr. Ouchterlony taught at a number of private schools around Ontario before settling in Toronto to become a teacher at (and later the Principal of) the Royal Conservatory. His works are mostly short vocal or instrumental pieces. His well-known *Carol Cantata*, which features carols in the styles of eight nations, was first performed in 1975 at Timothy Eaton Memorial Church in Toronto, where Dr. Ouchterlony was the organist and choirmaster.

SCHUBERT, Franz Peter (1797-1828). Austria. As a boy, Schubert learned violin from his father, piano from his older brother, and also sang as a chorister at the Imperial Chapel in Vienna. He made very little money as a young man and was quite dependent on the generosity of a large circle of devoted friends and patrons in Vienna. These patrons hosted evening musicales, called "Schubertiaden" because they only performed music by Schubert, often with Schubert accompanying the soloists on the piano. Although he composed a great deal of music for solo piano, he is perhaps best remembered for the more than 600 songs (called *Lieder* in German) that he composed using words by the great German poets of his time. Very sadly, Schubert died at the young age of 31.

SHARPE, Cecil James (1859-1924). Britain. Born in London, Sharpe held several organist posts and studied at Cambridge University. He devoted his entire live to preserving and reviving the performance of English folk songs and traditional dances. He collected, edited, and performed hundreds of pieces, and wrote books about them.

SMITH, Warren Storey (1885-1971). U.S.A. Born in Massachusetts, Smith studied piano in Boston and in 1922 joined the staff of the New England Conservatory where he taught until 1960. He worked as a music critic and editor for the *Boston Post* from 1923 to 1953. His compositions include a piano trio, piano solo pieces and songs.

*TELFER, Nancy (born 1950). Canada. A graduate  of The University of Western Ontario, Nancy Telfer now lives in Sunderland, Ontario where she composes full-time. Her many works for piano, voice, orchestra, and choir have been performed and featured at many festivals and conferences around the world. Telfer has always been interested in the outdoors and often draws inspiration from the beauty of nature. Many of her pieces are written with young performers in mind.

*VAN DER HOECK, Bert (born 1936). Canada.  Bert Van Der Hoek was born in the Netherlands and immigrated to Canada in 1952, settling in London, Ontario where he lives today. He is actively engaged in the retail music business and also works as a church musician. Though he has not composed a great deal of music, several of his anthems for junior and senior choirs have been published.

*WOOD, A. Dale (born 1944). Canada. Wood received his musical training at the University of Toronto. He currently lives in Georgetown, Ontario where he is a private piano teacher, choral conductor and arranger. For many years he worked closely with Barry Gosse and has arranged a number of his pieces.

Length of the examination: 20 minutes

Examination Fee: Please consult the current examination application form for the schedule of fees.

Co-requisite: None. There is NO written examination co-requisite for the awarding of the Grade 3 Practical Certificate.

NOTE: The Grade 3 examination is designed for younger singers. It is recommended that mature beginners enter the examination program at the Grade 4 level.

Candidates are expected to know all of the requirements and regulations for the examination as outlined in the current Conservatory Canada Voice Syllabus. In the event of a discrepancy between the current syllabus and the requirements set out below, the Syllabus must be considered definitive for examination purposes. No allowance can be made for candidates who misread or fail to follow any of the regulations and/or requirements for the examinations.

REQUIREMENTS & MARKING

Requirement	Total Marks
FOUR LIST PIECES	
TWO chosen from List A (Folksongs and all other songs before 1900)	24
TWO chosen from List B (Post 1900)	24
ONE SUPPLEMENTARY PIECE	8
VOCALISES: None required	0
TECHNICAL TESTS	16
SIGHT	
Rhythm	3
Singing	7
AURAL TESTS	10
VIVA VOCE	8
TOTAL POSSIBLE MARKS	100

NOTE: The examination program must include at least ONE piece by a Canadian composer. The Canadian piece may be chosen from the List Pieces OR as the Supplementary Piece.

PIECES

Candidates are required to perform FOUR PIECES contrasting in key, tempo, genre, era and subject: TWO pieces to be chosen from List A, and TWO pieces to be chosen from List B. Your choices must include four different composers. All pieces must be sung from memory. Pieces may be transposed to suit the compass of the candidate's voice.

SUPPLEMENTARY PIECE

Candidates must be prepared to sing from memory ONE SUPPLEMENTARY PIECE. This piece need not be from the Syllabus list, and may be chosen entirely at the discretion of the teacher and student. It may represent a period or style of piece not already included in the examination program, but which holds special interest for the candidate. You may use suitable pieces from the Broadway and musical theatre, to be performed WITHOUT movement, costume or props. The choice must be within the following guidelines:

1) The equivalent level of difficulty of the piece may be at a higher level, providing it is within the technical and musical grasp of the candidate.

2) Pieces below the equivalent of Grade 2 level are not acceptable.

3) The piece must be suitable for the candidate's voice and age.

4) The piece must be for solo voice (with or without piano accompaniment). Vocal duets are not acceptable.

Special approval is not required for the Supplementary Piece. However, poor suitability of choice may be reflected in the mark.

TECHNICAL EXERCISES

Candidates must be prepared to sing any or all of the exercises given below, in the following manner:

i)   Sung to vowels   **Ah [a], ay [e], ee [i], oh [o], oo [u]**

as requested by the examiner. Though the tonic sol-fa names may be used to learn these exercises, candidates may NOT sing using sol-fa names in the examination.

ii) Sung without accompaniment. A starting pitch will be given by the examiner. Exercises may be transposed from the keys given below into keys suitable to the candidate's voice range. The examiner may give a different starting pitch for each exercise.

iii) Metronome markings should be regarded as *minimum* speeds.

iv) Expression markings are not given for Grade 3 and are NOT required for the examination.

v)   All exercises must be sung in a single breath unless a breath mark is indicated in the score by a comma.

vi) A slur has been used to indicate legato singing. Staccato markings have been used to indicate staccato singing.

SIGHT READING

Candidates are required to perform at sight a) a rhythmic exercise and b) a passage of vocal score as described below. The candidate will be given a brief period to scan the score before beginning to sing. However, Candidates are not permitted to hum the melody while scanning. Candidates must perform the rhythm section without counting aloud. It is recommended that candidates choose a moderate tempo, maintain a steady beat, and avoid the unnecessary repetition caused by attempting to correct errors during the performance.

Before the candidate attempts to sing the vocal passage, the Examiner will play on the piano a I-IV-V-I chord progression (with the leading-note to tonic in the upper part) to establish the key and tonality. The tonic note will then be given.

a) *Rhythm*	*b)* *Vocal Passage*
To tap, clap or play on one note (at the candidate's choice) a simple rhythm. Length 4 bars Time signature 2/4, 3/4. 4/4 Note values whole,1/2, dotted 1/2, 1/4, 1/8 & dotted 1/4 followed by 1/8 Rest values whole, 1/2, 1/4, 1/8	To sing at sight a simple unaccompanied melody, within a range of six notes and within the limits of the great (or grand) staff. The melody begins on the tonic note. Candidates may use either any vowel of their choice or the tonic sol-fa names. Major keys only up to an including 2 sharps or flats Length 4-8 bars Time signature 2/4, 3/4, 4/4 Note values whole, 1/2, dotted 1/2, 1/4 Rest values whole, 1/2, 1/4 Melodic Intervals 2nds, 3rds, 5ths

Example: a) Rhythm

Example: b) Vocal Passage

AURAL TESTS

The candidate will be required:

i) to clap back the rhythmic pattern of a short melody in 2/4, 3/4 or 4/4 time, consisting of whole, half, dotted half, quarter, dotted quarter and eighth notes, after it has been played twice by the Examiner at the keyboard. Following is the approximate level of difficulty:

ii) to identify *major* or *minor* triad chords played once by the Examiner in solid form and in close, root position.

iii) to identify *major* or *harmonic minor* or *melodic minor* scales played once by the Examiner, ascending and descending, at a moderate tempo.

iv)   the *major* **or** *minor* common [four-note] chord of any key will be played once by the Examiner in broken form slowly, ascending and descending. The chord will be in root position. One of the four notes will then be re-sounded for the candidate to identify, by saying, at the candidate's choice:

         EITHER (1)   its interval number [1, 3, 5, 8],
         OR   (2)   its tonic sol-fa name.

VIVA VOCE

Candidates must be prepared to give verbal answers to questions on the FOUR List pieces selected for the examination. Candidates must ensure that all teaching notes and other written comments are removed from the score before the examination. The questions will include the following elements:

i)   to find and explain all of the signs (including clefs, time signatures, key signatures, accidentals, etc.), articulation markings (legato, staccato, accents, phrase or slur markings, etc.), dynamic and tempo markings, and other musical terms as they may be found in the four selected pieces.

ii)   without reference to the score, to give the title, key and composer of the piece.

iii)   to explain the meaning of the title of the piece.

iv)   To play on the piano a *major* triad (root position only) on any white *note within two octaves above or below middle C*, as requested by the Examiner. The candidate should also be prepared to transform the same triad into a *minor* triad by lowering the third. Candidates will not be required to read this triad from score.

O CANADA

*Written in French by Adolphe-Basile Routhier (1839-1920) in Quebec City and first performed there in 1880
to a musical setting by Calixa Lavallée. Translated into English in 1908 by Robert Stanley Wier (1856-1926).
Approved as Canada's national anthem by the Parliament of Canada in 1967 and adopted officially in 1980.*

Adolphe-Basile Routhier
English version by Robert Stanley Wier

*Calixa Lavallée
(1842-1891)
arr. D.F. Cook

CONSERVATORY CANADA™

Conservatory Canada conducts piano examinations throughout Canada from the Grade 1 level to the professional Associate Diploma level.

Please direct all examination enquiries to:

Office of the Registrar
Conservatory Canada
45 King Street, Suite 61
London, Ontario, Canada
N6A 1B8

Telephone: 519-433-3147
Toll free in Canada: 1-800-461-5367

Fax: 519-433-7404

Email: officeadmin@conservatorycanada.ca